I0489935

Six Sigma Service

By Ade Asefeso MCIPS MBA

ISBN-13: 978-1499365306
ISBN-10: 1499365306

Publisher: AA Global Sourcing Ltd
Website: http://www.aaglobalsourcing.com

Table of Contents

Disclaimer

This publication is designed to provide competent and reliable information regarding the subject matter covered. However, it is sold with the understanding that the author and publisher are not engaged in rendering professional advice. The authors and publishers specifically disclaim any liability that is incurred from the use or application of contents of this book.

If you purchased this book without a cover you should be aware that this book may have been stolen property and reported as "unsold and destroyed" to the publisher. In this case neither the author nor the publisher has received any payment for this "stripped book."

Dedication

This book is dedicated to my family and friends who seems to have been sent here to teach me something about who I am supposed to be. They have nurtured me, challenged me, and even opposed me.... But at every juncture has taught me!

This book is dedicated to my lovely boys, Thomas, Michael and Karl. Teaching them to manage their finance will give them the lives they deserve. They have taught me more about life, presence, and energy management than anything I have done in my life.

Chapter 1: Introduction

Six Sigma is all about quality improvement and was first pioneered by Motorola in the 1980s. Over the last few years, this methodology has received much recognition and several companies have adopted it in order to meet their targets. Six Sigma's clientele include a long list of well-established manufacturers like General Motors, Ford Motor Co., GE, Honeywell and many more. However, there are still many non-manufacturing companies that have come to the conclusion that Six Sigma will not work for them. This is because Six Sigma was originally developed for helping the manufacturing industry. Organizations such as health care systems, financial service providers and educational systems all doubt the usefulness of Six Sigma.

Why the service sector feels that Six Sigma is not for them

The most obvious reason why service companies keep away from Six Sigma is because they perceive it as a manufacturing tool. Service organizations feel that because their companies have a large amount of human work force, there are no measurable defects to be corrected. However, experts say this is not true. A recent survey has shown that service companies that have invested in Six Sigma are all saving millions of dollars for every project. Human resources makes up a large part of all service organizations. To conquer this problem, leaders of the industry can be trained in Six Sigma to balance their employment expertise with statistics-based analytical tools.

The fear of metrics is another obstacle that stands in the way of the service sector and Six Sigma. Most people feel that Six Sigma sounds too technical. The importance of metrics is to give an insight into the business working processes. Service based companies need to focus all their attention on developing Six Sigma projects that specialize in their business needs like customer and cash generation. Convincing the service sector about the merits of taking up Six Sigma has proven to be a big challenge. Most service companies still believe that Six Sigma can only benefit the manufacturing industry.

How Six Sigma can benefit the service industry

Six Sigma goes into the details of improving customer service, generating business expansion and gaining knowledge about the service sectors business processes. Most service industries revolve around areas of finance, human resources and sales and marketing. Hence, Six Sigma delves deeply into the subject of soft skills. Six Sigma can be applied to a company that provides housekeeping services. Firstly, the companies working processes would need to be understood. Using the DMIAC method or the define-measure-improve-analyze-control method, Six Sigma can definitely implement quality in any industry. As the main aim of this methodology is to reduce defects, the first step would be detecting the particular defect. Secondly, data will be collected to observe how, why and how often these defects occur. Next, the Six Sigma team implements an outstanding employees method of working as the normal method for all employees. Finally, new employees are taught the correct techniques.

Six Sigma is useful in the field of sales and marketing as well. According to Six Sigma data, during sales, too much face time with a customer can prove to be counter-productive. Changing this process can result in an increase in the percentage of sales per product. Other industries that Six Sigma has assisted in the past are the financial service sector, insurance companies, management companies, educational institutions, high-tech companies, state agencies and many more.

Chapter 2: Diagnostic X-ray and Lean Six Sigma

As Lean Six Sigma's popularity grows in the services industries, so can the disappointing results. An upfront diagnostic X-ray helps companies get more from their efforts.

Lean Six Sigma was originally devised to eliminate waste and improve manufacturing quality to no more than 3.4 defects per million opportunities. But now the method made popular at companies like General Electric Co., Xerox Corp., and Johnson & Johnson is increasingly finding a home in the services industry.

We have seen banks use Lean Six Sigma to support their growth strategy; financial services companies to put mergers back on track; energy companies to lower costs; telecommunications companies to improve customer service; and retailers to increase efficiency while boosting customer service in the store. But Lean Six Sigma's growing popularity in the services industry masks a downside.

Many organizations have trained and deployed legions of Lean Six Sigma experts known as black belts only to see little value result from their work. In our recent management survey of 170 companies, 80 percent say their Lean Six Sigma efforts are failing to drive the anticipated value, and 74 percent say they are not gaining the expected competitive edge because they haven't achieved their savings targets.

Drilling deeper, we discovered that mobilizing large and costly squads of black belts in some cases actually slows performance improvement efforts. Managers are unsure how best to deploy the Lean Six Sigma experts and too often black belts treat all problems, big and small, with the same approach, resulting in less-effective solutions. Moreover, they fail to prioritize the improvements that will make the biggest difference.

This last issue is particularly vexing to companies as they search for ways to reduce costs or boost revenues. While Lean Six Sigma can be excellent at remedying obvious maladies like call-centre bottlenecks, it is less adept at uncovering the hidden sources of pain and identifying and sizing the largest opportunities for cost savings, waste reduction, or revenue generation. It is unnecessary and wasteful to run every process through Lean Six Sigma. Knowing where to focus before unleashing the black belts can make all the difference.

Companies that are yielding the biggest gains from Lean Six Sigma are deploying an upfront diagnostic X-ray to help them identify the most critical opportunities. Performed by a small advance team of black belts, the diagnostic X-ray consists of three steps.

1. Enterprise Value Stream Mapping, in which the X-ray team scans the enterprise and maps its primary processes to identify the biggest opportunities to reduce cost by reducing wasted time and materials.

2. Benchmarking, in which the performance of processes is measured against internal and external benchmarks to gauge shortcomings and establish improvement targets.

3. Prioritizing, in which the X-ray team determines which process improvements will yield the greatest results when the Lean Six Sigma teams are deployed.

Only after the X-ray has identified the most pressing issues do companies begin the traditional five-step Lean Six Sigma DMAIC process - Define, Measure, Analyze, Improve, and Control on the targeted areas.

Chapter 3: Diagnostic X-ray and Lean Six Sigma Methodology

This methodology paid off for a major UK insurance company that found itself at a crossroads. Plans to grow its market share by 150 percent were threatened by market changes that put new pressure on profits. The firm knew its internal processes were inefficient, but prior efforts to streamline them had failed. So, the insurer decided to take a diagnostic X-ray of its business to determine where to focus its efforts. By first examining its processes within a single business unit, the X-ray team was able to compare similar processes used by other business units to create benchmarks and set performance targets and priorities for reducing waste. The result was a dramatic reduction in annual processing time and revenue savings.

1. Enterprise Value Stream Mapping

The first move taken by the X-ray team is to develop a map of the operation's processes and the costs associated with them. The goal is to understand what activities a company performs, the source of its biggest expenses, and where inefficiencies or performance gaps exist. For instance, during the mapping stage, the insurance company's team started by creating a business process fact base, which involved looking at, processes from end to end; everything from account setup to claims handling and gathering data on 189 activities. An analysis showed that there were seven major steps in the value chain.

Each step then was broken out to look at time spent and staffing levels. This break-down helped the company zero in on major inefficiencies. The company found that it was spending the same amount of time and money on every claim be it for a highly valued customer like a global corporation, or a single individual; with the value stream maps in hand; the team could see where improved performance would deliver the greatest and fastest cost savings.

2. Benchmarking

Determining how much performance might be improved is the purpose of the second step of the X-ray. The aim of this phase is to establish valid benchmarks, both internal and external, for each process to identify appropriate performance-improvement targets. Benchmarking was key to the dramatic reduction in processing time and cost savings achieved by the insurance company.

Using the results of value stream mapping, the X-ray team at the insurance company then established internal benchmarks by examining how various business units carried out similar processes. They found costly differences. For example, in one unit, the claims-handling process represented 11 percent of total costs, while at another business unit it was only 6 percent. The X-ray team found that the "placement" process gathering customer information, placing insurance, issuing certificates, handing over processing to the back office, and chasing client payments took twice as long in one business unit as it did in another. Armed with this knowledge, the company could establish valid performance targets for its less-efficient processes and develop standardized processing times.

Lean Six Sigma for the services industry benchmarking also helped the team track its costs by activity an exercise that allowed the company to better understand client risk. The company was able to see where it made money, exposing the most to least-profitable business units. The cost curve starkly showed how the company could tailor service to better align costs to what clients value, breaking customers into three segments based on overall profitability.

3. Prioritizing

In this final phase of the X-ray, the team decides which problems to pursue in which order. For the insurance company, this meant plotting the value of solutions against how difficult they did be to implement. At the top of the list: three opportunities for boosting revenues and cost savings, while also more effectively meeting customer needs. With its priorities firmly established, the black belts embarked on the Lean Six Sigma process.

First, the company set out to re-price some policies charging more to clients that were expensive to serve, and raising prices for smaller clients that demanded tailored service. Within the first year, re-pricing alone earned the insurer an additional 10 percent of profits.

Second, the black belts worked on a series of organizational changes like standardizing the processing times across business units boosting profits by a further 10 percent.

Third, over the next 30 months, the insurer invested in technology upgrades that included sophisticated cost-modelling tools. Overtime, the investment paid off by allowing business units to calculate such details as how many hours employees need to spend on gold standard clients versus other customer segments. The cost analysis changed staffing assumptions, like how large a sales team it needed. Ultimately, IT investments helped deliver a final 30 percent profit increase.

Chapter 4: Putting the X-ray to Work

The UK insurance company's experience demonstrates how a technique originally designed to improve efficiency and quality on the factory floor is finding a home in the services industry. As Lean Six Sigma spreads to new industries, it is being deployed to help companies meet a range of new objectives. When paired with the diagnostic X-ray, the Lean concept becomes an even more powerful tool, showing companies how they can do everything from spending less on equipment to redesigning stores for efficiency to performing a better job of stocking and replenishing inventory. The following five case studies illustrate the breadth of the diagnostic X-ray's potential.

1. A bank supports its growth strategy

A major Australian commercial bank wanted to take advantage of a market shift that was pushing more business in its direction. But it wouldn't be able to handle larger, more complex loan applications unless it overhauled credit processes at every level of the organization from loan processing to credit policies to the sales force and credit approval teams.

The bank needed new capabilities that would increase the speed, accuracy, and efficiency of credit processes and decision making. The protracted loan approval process was driving away new investments from valued customers who needed and expected quick action. Value stream mapping of the bank's credit processes revealed major trouble spots in the bank's systems, including a lack of uniformity in loan approvals. Too often, credit officers made judgment-based, instead of rule-based, loan decisions. Also, all loans large or small had to move through the same initial layers of approval, with 20 percent sent through a more rigorous screening, even when the bank was familiar with a client's risk history. Finally, the process was riddled with inefficiencies and downtime and many applications required reworking due to errors. During a series of workshops, loan managers who dealt directly with clients expressed their frustration with credit approval officers who often failed to update them about a loan's status. As a result of poor communication and delays, loan managers found it harder to win new business.

The bank used benchmarking to determine how long, where, and why loans were stuck in the approval process, as well as the reasons behind rejections. By comparing systems at different branches, the team could see which ones were working and what differences resulted in improvements. For example, one branch had expedited its loan approvals by placing a more experienced credit approval officer on the floor to work with loan managers. This partnering helped customers get a better sense of both timing and approval odds.

With mapping and benchmarking results in hand, the bank prioritized a list of high-value opportunities for Lean Six Sigma. Top priorities; developing a fast track for lower-risk loans, standardizing processes, and improving risk assessment and borrowing a lesson from the branch that was able to speed up loan approvals, credit approval officers would work with loan managers on a customized application process that included such steps as asking a customer up front for specific information.

The diagnostic X-ray helped the bank focus its black belts on opportunities that promised the best results. With the improvements in place, new business is fuelling growth rates at 2.5 times the market. Almost 50 percent of loan applications now go through the new fast-track approval process, which has translated into a 30 percent quicker approval time for customers.

Approval times now take 3 - 6 days less, ranging from 7-14 days, down from 10 - 20 days. With more experienced credit officers working in the field, the number of loans requiring more time-intensive reviews has dropped from 20 percent to 5 percent and there are fewer errors streamlining and standardizing processes has cut by 25 percent the number of applications that need reworking.

2. A mobile phone provider improves customer service and also cuts costs

A leading European mobile phone company in a highly competitive marketplace knew it had to beef up customer service to prevent competitors from winning away its customers.

At the root of the problem was the company's customer service centre. Operators were swamped with calls, they had a poor track record for resolving customer problems, and the call-centre was operating with a limited budget. The company needed a two-pronged solution; a new call-centre strategy that would transform the centre into a revenue generator; and the ability to zero in on the most critical initiatives to improve customer service.

The diagnostic X-ray laid the groundwork for the Lean Six Sigma work that would develop both solutions. It exposed key call-centre inefficiencies, which in many cases were driving customer defections. The X-ray showed that the biggest cost saver would be to redesign systems so operators could resolve problems on the first call, allowing the company to reduce staffing and to turn the call centre into a revenue generator, the X-ray process used customer and competitor surveys to create benchmarks for identifying three distinct customer groups based on their customer value. That ultimately led to creating service.

Lean Six Sigma for the services industry plans for each customer segment. By knowing where to focus its efforts, the mobile phone operator's new call-centre strategy has improved customer service and started generating revenue. The company is on track to save 25 percent of its operating costs in less than three years.

3. Saving a merger: Figuring out who does what best

A major financial institution used the diagnostic X-ray and Lean Six Sigma to resolve cultural differences that threatened the success of a recent merger. When a merchant bank acquired the market leader in its segment, management couldn't reach a consensus on how to run the merged business. The former competitors used vastly different business practices and processes. The resulting culture clash was driving top talent out of the door. By employing the diagnostic X-ray, management was able to build a consensus around merged operating practices and quickly prioritize high-value areas for improvement.

The key to resolving the culture clash was developing a "best of both worlds" approach. In the value-stream mapping phase, they looked at loans both institutions had reviewed. The comparison allowed bank officials to see how differences in their processes affected loan approvals and client relationships.

The mapping uncovered a key difference in how the two banks handled more-complex, higher-risk deals. While the larger merchant bank did a better job assessing the risk of bigger deals, approvals took as much as two times longer. Even on easier deals, the approval process was slow. By comparison, the acquired bank was smoother and faster at loan approvals, and was better at customer service but its deals typically were smaller.

To get a sense of the industry standard, the diagnostic team benchmarked the banks against competitors' approval processes for deals over $50 million. They discovered that the acquiring bank had many unnecessary steps, especially for easier deals. Customer interviews revealed that while large loan approvals were handled appropriately, the bank needed to take a tip from its acquired partner and improve customer relations by better managing the expectations of its highly-valued private equity clients.

Once areas for improvement were identified, the bank prioritized them by asking "What are the two or three high-impact, easy-to-implement ways to improve the loan approval process and retain talent?" Since pay raises were not in consideration, the bank looked at changes that would streamline the process without dramatically changing the way employees were accustomed to working.

The answer; a loan approval system with a path that allows for two choices; a simpler route with fewer hurdles for low-risk deals; a more rigorous, standardized process for more complex deals. The solution incorporated the acquired bank's ease and predictability with the acquiring bank's sophistication for handling larger deals. To let the market-place know that the merged bank could handle both higher-risk private equity loans as well as smaller ones with the same speed and dependability, it sent out a newsletter showcasing recent loans and the time it took to get them done.

By using the diagnostic X-ray, the two banks built a strong business case for merging their two cultures. The concrete data and specifics helped them acknowledge relative strengths and agree on which processes required improvements. Black belts then went to work using Lean Six Sigma's DMAIC methodology, drilling down on specific improvement initiatives and developing metrics to ensure continuous results. This "best of both worlds" approach has allowed the merged entity to increase its average deal size by 35 percent, and by streamlining processes, management is able to quickly move applications through the approval process.

4. A retailer uncovers small fixes for substantial gains

A US big-box retail market leader needed to stave off competition from general merchandise discounters to keep its strong growth on track. But the cost of its solution making stores more customer friendly was skyrocketing faster than it was delivering results.

The retailer needed a customer-focused strategy that it could afford over the long haul. The diagnostic X-ray in advance of

24

Lean Six Sigma played a crucial supporting role, uncovering ways to cut costs that would be invisible to customers.

The diagnostic X-ray team used value stream mapping for up to 100 operations to determine how many hours were spent each week on routine tasks, everything from opening and closing stores, pricing, taking inventory, restocking shelves, and filling orders placed through the retailer's website. Tasks with high numbers relative to the activity's importance went to the top of the target list for improvements. Armed with the list of potential targets, the diagnostic team headed to stores where they observed processes looking for those that seemed ripe for streamlining. The team surveyed employees and conducted internal benchmarking by comparing systems, store to store. No process was too small for review like the existing process of requiring employees to fill out a special form each time a customer requested price matching. Employees explained that the time-consuming form never was looked at again. Also on the target list was the inefficient system for filling online orders. While the retailer was encouraging customers to place orders on its website for pickup at a nearby store, the system for getting orders into customers' hands was unreliable and time consuming. The team found out why; unless an employee was stationed at a computer, the store had no way of knowing when an order arrived. There were further inefficiencies when it came to filling the order. Items were not placed near the pickup area in any particular order, causing delays as employees searched for the right product.

The X-ray team examined another process it had red-flagged; the system used to keep a steady stream of high-profit items on store shelves. It was more important to have a $100 high-margin core item in stock than a $5 accessory. By watching employees and checking merchandise holes on shelves, the team realized that workers were not following a weekly plan for restocking inventory. When asked why, employees said the plan was so detailed, it felt impossible to get through the entire inventory in a week.

Back at corporate headquarters, the team prioritized tasks for retooling by estimating the value of each opportunity measured against the cost of implementation. What is impressive is that instead of a few big home runs, the retailer found $50 million in annual cost reductions from small process changes. Top priorities included:

a. Redesigning the restocking calendar so employees could easily see which products to check at what times each day throughout a month. Projected annual savings was $10 million.

b. Eliminating those time consuming customer forms for $3 million annually in savings ($2.3 million from labour and $800,000 from paper).

c. Fixing the online order pickup process. By adding new ways to ensure that the store was aware when an order was received, and changing how and where items were stored for easy retrieval, the retailer could save another $1.2 million.

d. Standardizing the daily setup of cash register drawers. The company found it could save another $700,000 annually simply by knowing how much change is needed.

When the retailer finally unleashed its black belts, the diagnostic allowed it to focus immediately on creating results that matter.

5. An energy leader discovers a savings windfall and fends off competitors

A leading UK energy company saddled with $1 billion in operating expenses needed to improve its cost performance to protect its market leadership. To curb customer defections and better compete, the company sought to transform its business processes, which were riddled with inefficiencies. The company decided to increase its odds of success by taking a diagnostic X-ray before unleashing its Lean Six Sigma black belts.

By performing a detailed mapping of costs related to all aspects of customer service from pursuing new customers, setting up accounts, measuring energy use, and collecting payments the diagnostic team developed a detailed analysis of cost-saving opportunities. The biggest one was a surprise. During the mapping phase, the company determined how often its representatives read a meter; then in the benchmarking phase, the company found that nearly 50 percent of its meter-reading expenses were avoidable. Most of the opportunity came from simply reducing the number of times it reads a meter. No team of black belts was even required in this case; the diagnostic X-ray convinced the company it didn't need to use the Lean Six Sigma methodology to fix its meter-reading operation.

As it prioritized other cost-saving opportunities, the company found additional ways to score several quick wins. By more effectively targeting new customers and reducing call-centre costs, it could trim customer acquisition expenses automating routine calls alone would save over $5 million annually. It could trim support costs by 20 percent to 30 percent with a redesign of billing, payment and debt-collection processes. In the end, the detailed X-ray of core processes showed the company how it could reduce 30 percent of its total costs, while at the same time more effectively competing for new customers and improving customer service. Once the black belts set to work on these initiatives, the energy leader was on track to achieve stronger cost performance and its long-term competitive strategy. Such is the power of the diagnostic X-ray.

Chapter 5: Is it Sufficient?

The purpose of this chapter is to explore the more detailed concepts surrounding Six Sigma and to determine whether it's a sufficient approach in the understanding and improvement of business processes in service organizations.

In order to evaluate the usefulness and appropriateness of applying Six Sigma to the improvement of service processes, it's essential to understand some of the basic concepts of that discipline. In its purest form, Six Sigma is all about eliminating defects from a manufactured product. The approach taken to do this comprised of five phases (or steps or activities). These are summed up in the acronym DMAIC. DMAIC stands for Define, Measure, Analyze, Improve, and Control.

1. Define the problem and what the customers require.
2. Measure the defects and process operation.
3. Analyze the data and discover causes of the problem.
4. Improve the process to remove causes of defects.
5. Control the process to make sure defects don't recur.

In organizations where any kind of structure for approaching process improvement is missing, these activities probably make a lot of sense. In fact, if combined with other concepts and approaches, there is nothing wrong with these activities. The question to answer is, "Are they sufficient and appropriate for service organizations?"

I have met and spoken with several people who either are Black Belts or worked in organizations that had several Black Belts. Those that worked for service organizations, without exception, said that Six Sigma, as it is structured for success in manufacturing, didn't work for them. They were able to take some concepts from Six Sigma and mix them together with concepts from other business process management frameworks to create success stories.

There is an argument that it isn't Six Sigma that creates the successes; it's the combination of some of the elements of Six Sigma with some really good process management strategies like executive buy-in, dedicating a significant budget to training, and tying the results from projects to executive compensation. Any really good framework or methodology will (should) incorporate these concepts.

The purpose of this chapter is not to question the usefulness of Six Sigma but to create a discussion around whether or not it alone is a sufficient choice for organizations in the service sector. Taking a look at each of the concerns below, we can deconstruct each of the success stories for Six Sigma and see how they became successes.

There are a multitude of concepts surrounding Six Sigma that make it a questionable approach for service processes. They include:
1. Its focus is on "defects" to the exclusion of other aspects of a service process that are critical to success.
2. It assumes that control points are in place and that defects only occur at the beginning or end of the process (based on types of metrics and when they are collected).
3. It was designed specifically for a manufacturing environment.
4. It focuses on activities or pieces of processes instead of the whole process or value chain.

5. It ignores the concepts around adaptability/flexibility.
6. It does not focus on any stakeholder other than "Customer".
7. It ignores the people aspect of process.

It ignores the "guide" and "enabler" concepts, e.g., policy, procedures, regulations, knowledge, experience, and events.

Focus on Defects

Six Sigma, what is it? Sigma in Greek stands for "standard deviation." Six Sigma is 99.9997% perfection. The main focus of a Six Sigma discipline is on statistics, not "gut-feel." It's really all about how to collect and analyze statistics to determine the defect rate of whatever is being measured. In a manufacturing environment, it's much easier to identify and measure defects. When following Six Sigma, most of this information would be gathered from efforts called "voice of the customer."

However, in a service environment it's much more difficult to identify what a "defect" is and to measure how much it matters to the customer (or that we "feel" it matters to the customer). "Is it Cake or is it Clean?" I discussed this dilemma. In short, when you are making a cake, there are very well-defined criteria for whether it's a quality cake or, in fact, if it contains defects. But when you are cleaning something (like your house) how do you define "clean"? How do you quantify clean for the cleaner? How do you define the defects of clean?

This has become much more difficult because what we are trying to define is an intangible concept. My definition of clean and my house cleaner's definition of clean may not be the same ... and frequently are not. Lately, I have been giving the job of cleaning the house to my 16 year-old son and have realized that his definition of clean is also different from mine. Some of this is simply due to a lack of experience. But a lot of it is based on perception and acceptance criteria and effort involved.

What I have come to realize is that, when trying to define defects, it depends on who the customer is. Most service organizations put a lot of effort into gathering statistics for customer satisfaction, but "customer satisfaction" can vary depending on the customer's last experience. The company could be providing the same level of service and some other variable has created a negative experience for the customer. So, if the company were trying to collect defect data, would there be a defect in the service or the circumstance?

The dilemma of the intangible service makes it frustrating, if not impossible, to define and collect data for defects. That is not to suggest that service organizations do not need to understand this concept, but the reality of implementing a true Six Sigma calculation may cost more than the return on the investment. That takes us back to the Quality Dilemma of the '80s and '90s where quality programs were found to not be cost effective.

Organizations that attempt the Six Sigma approach for their services find themselves forced to focus only on the tangible aspects of the process such as transaction volumes, error rates, re-work, and time consumed. The danger is in the intangibles, such as ability to adapt and change, to respond to changing customer expectations, etc. It's the inadaptability of service processes that is hurting many service organizations, and yet this is one area that Six Sigma, in its truest form, ignores completely.

For those organizations that provide services, what makes them successful is not how few defects they produce but rather (on a more positive note) the number of things they do right. Staying focused on doing things right and doing them better will eventually eliminate the defects.

Specifically Designed for Manufacturing

Manufacturing-based organizations desperately needed something in the late '80s and '90s to fix the mistakes of the '70s that had almost completely devastated the manufacturing industry in the U.S. Motorola was one of the first to move away from the traditional approach to solving manufacturing problems that invested large amounts of money into yet another quality program that might or might not work. Instead, they started looking outward to the customer and inward to their own processes to resolve their quality issues. What Six Sigma provided Motorola was an attainable, very aggressive quality goal of almost defect-free products. The metrics for this were easily attainable and fairly easy to track and collect because of the manufacturing environment.

So, other companies recognizing that the success at Motorola was accomplished without an overinvestment in the "Japanese" type quality programs jumped on the bandwagon, eager to replicate Motorola's success. GE (a mixed organization that contained both the manufacturing environment and the service environment) jumped in with both feet and, as a result, was also able to attain some major successes. However, at GE they were already finding that they needed to incorporate some significant changes to the

Motorola approach. The most significant change was tying the results to executive compensation.

In addition to creating a monetary incentive, CEO Jack Welch also told management that if they wanted to be promoted to a senior management position within GE, they must start Black-Belt (and even Green Belt) training by January 1, 1998.

GE already had a program in place called "work-out" that created an environment within the company for employees to question "the way things work."

GE invested $250 million in training and trained over 64,000 out of a total workforce of 222,000. This created an environment where a large portion of the workforce had a very clear understanding of the Six Sigma concepts. Such an understanding is critical to the success of any process improvement project, whatever method is used.

Some would say that GE did everything right. But it wasn't Six Sigma that created the success; it was the management support and buy-in, the training, and the push from the very top of the organization that made this successful. I would counter that there are a number of other, less well-known frameworks that could be just as successful from an improvement perspective and, in fact, cost much less, resulting in a much higher ROI. The Six Sigma training is some of the most expensive of its kind.

What made these success stories was not Six Sigma as it's strictly applied in manufacturing but rather a collection of other common sense factors.

Measures for Six Sigma

In discussions with Black Belts and with further research, I found it very interesting that the entire focus of a Six Sigma project was on effectiveness and efficiency. I could not find anything that suggested organizations should try to collect data on and measure adaptability. Almost all of my consulting work is with service organizations, and in the last 3 years I have not had one organization that didn't list adaptability or flexibility as one of their major concerns regarding the services they provided. They readily recognize that when they are beaten by their competition, it's because they were too slow to respond to the market.

In addition, the granularity of the measures needed to accurately calculate Sigma are not readily available in service type organizations, and it may not be feasible to collect when the cost of collecting them is factored into the project.

Six Sigma as an Activity vs. Process Focus

Most organizations approach Six Sigma as a problem-solving approach, rather than as strategic improvement or business transformation. This can prove to be a very disruptive approach, particularly in a service organization. In providing services it's more likely for processes to cross several organizational boundaries therefore, an approach that focuses on solving problems in just a single area/function in an organization can cause many more problems than it solves because it is simply moving the problem from one part of the organization to another without really eliminating it or discovering its cause.

This also makes change management much more difficult because it addresses change in small increments, in isolated parts of the organization. Change management experts will quickly point out that "real" change management is only effective when it encompasses as much of the culture of the organization as is feasible. For example, GE was successful in its Six Sigma projects because it was a cultural change that crossed all boundaries of the organization. GE already had a program called "work-out" in place that crossed many of the normal barriers that cause problems in other companies.

In order to be truly successful, a process improvement project must follow this example. It needs to look at the whole process, not just small portions of it, applying common "fire fighting" techniques. The fire might be extinguished but nothing has addressed how to prevent it from occurring again in the future or from breaking out in a different part of the organization.

It's only when LEAN concepts are incorporated with Six Sigma that the idea of the "value chain" is considered. Many, if not all, of the success stories in LEAN Six Sigma for Service can be attributed to the fact that the focus of the improvement project is on a much broader view of the process.

The "Voice of the Customer" (VOC) is the Focus of Everything

In a Six Sigma project, the "voice of the customer" is everything. It's used to define defects and to determine project definitions. Most organizations probably don't give enough attention to the "voice of the customer." However, there are numerous other stakeholders in an organization that also impact success. For example, other external stakeholders include suppliers, financial institutions, government regulators, community, and competitors. There are also internal stakeholders that should be considered, such as other processes, business units, and staff.

The idea that projects are chosen based almost solely on the "voice of the customer" is concerning. What happens to the expectations of all the other stakeholder groups? What opportunities have been missed due to this focus? All stakeholder expectations should be understood and factored into the decision. Not all stakeholders carry the same weight when these evaluations are made, but it is important that an organization understands the impact to those stakeholders.

In addition, the idea of how the work of a project "aligns" to all the areas of an organization is also important. Consideration should be given to whether the perceived problem to be solved is the result of a poor alignment of technology to organization structure, or organization structure to strategy or knowledge or perhaps even capabilities.

Sometimes process problems are all about capabilities. Given a different set of capabilities in the workforce, the process problem might be 90% solved. In a Six Sigma project it is highly likely this issue might not ever be identified, resulting in continuous fire fighting.

What Makes Six Sigma Seem Successful?

1. Highly-visible, top-down management commitment to the initiative.
2. A measurement system (metrics) to track progress.

3. Internal and External Benchmarking of the organization's products, services, and processes.
4. Stretch goals to focus people on changing the process by which the work gets done, rather than "tweaking" the existing process.
5. Educating all levels of the organization.
6. Success stories to demonstrate how the approach is applied and the results.
7. Champions and Black Belts to promote the initiatives and to provide the necessary planning, teaching, coaching, and consulting at all levels of the organization.

There is actually nothing wrong with any of the above points. The problem is that none of it is part of the Six Sigma approach. These are all the things that need to happen outside of the concepts of Six Sigma, and it's inappropriate to attribute an organization's success with process improvement to Six Sigma under these circumstances. That success is due to the implementation of process change supported by all the elements mentioned above, not due to anything that Six Sigma specifically brings to the project.

After discussions with Black Belts and further research into the topic of Six Sigma, it seems apparent that it is not the discipline of using the Six Sigma defects calculation or the DMAIC framework that helps organizations, especially service organizations, make those really incredible improvements to process. It calls for a much broader approach than Six Sigma, such as one that incorporates LEAN, which considers the whole value chain and not just pieces and parts of it.

There are a multitude of process management concepts that suggest that it is important for an approach to include things like process architectures and alignment of the organization and the expectations of other stakeholders in addition to the customer. Incorporating executive compensation as part of the motivation is a tremendous critical success factor. There is a saying that "we get what we pay for." It is apparent that, if executives are motivated and the organization invests literally millions of dollars into training its people, the likelihood that something in an organization will change is dramatically increased. However, none of that happens if an organization is implementing just a Six Sigma framework.

This chapter has examined concepts of Six Sigma that make it a questionable approach for service processes. There seems to be a legitimate concern for trying to apply Six Sigma concepts in service organizations. Morphing something that was developed and intended for use in a manufacturing environment; where there are tangible products to monitor for defects and where measures are collected constantly into something to use in service organizations; where almost everything that happens is intangible and few (if any) measures exist seems like a lot of hard work for very little, or no, gain.

A better approach for a service organization is to adopt a good process management framework that starts with the strategy of the organization, defines all the stakeholders and their expectations, and then aligns all of that with all aspects of the organization (such as organization structure, technology, knowledge, capabilities, etc.). Then, the organization can develop a definition of its processes and conduct an assessment of the health of those processes. Next comes priority setting on which processes will provide the greatest return (ROI) when improved and a program management strategy set up to manage those projects. Apply the common sense approach of defining the project, understanding the current situation, capturing measures to support those conclusions, and analyzing the process using root cause and value-add techniques. Then, based on the results of all of this work, improvements to the processes can be proposed and implemented, the progress of the implementation monitored, and any corrections made where necessary.

In the final analysis, Six Sigma does seem to bring a discipline to those that have none. The basic approach of Six Sigma define, measure, analyze, improve, and control should be applied to every process improvement project. The larger question is, "Is it sufficient?" The conclusion is you should be able to make-up your mind once you finish reading this book.

Chapter 6: Six Sigma for Non-Manufacturing Sector

The Six Sigma revolution has systematically taken over various sectors of the industry owing to its methodological process variations of working towards achieving targets and eliminating any defects occurring in them throughout the procedure. Since it aims at providing top class service and works towards being a reliable and valuable enterprise for its customers, it has made an entry into areas such as banking, telecommunications, marketing, insurance, healthcare, software and construction.

Range of Six Sigma

Earlier the scope of Six Sigma was limited to manufacturing processes, which accounted for only two percent of the United States industry. Nowadays, the non-manufacturing corporations such as IT management, Finance, Human Resource, Sales and services have also realized the need for top quality and are implementing Six Sigma to improve their service value.

The non-manufacturing course follows the 5S code under Six Sigma system, which is Sort, Set in order, Shine, Standardize and Sustain. The company requires classifying various items and then eliminates the ones, which are not related to the process and red tags them. This clears space for a much-required process that needs to be implemented on a daily basis. Secondly, it defines a work path for all individuals, decreasing the wastage of labour and focusing on specified details of the job. Polishing the work skills and worker's knowledge is also focused on to keep the work force updated with the latest developments of the world in fields of science, technology, economics, finance and others.

Need for Six Sigma in Non-Manufacturing Ground

The non-manufacturing corporations mainly deal with customers, suppliers and clients on a routine basis. It encompasses those soft processes that are the driving force behind the production and distribution of every product and service. The soft processes are human centric and each situation is a unique case hence, it requires scientific application to reduce and manage the variances. This necessitates standardization, as the quantity of automated equipment is less and human resource is greater.

Performance and Efficiency

Efficiency is another factor which demands Six Sigma application. The managers are required to think and formulate utility processes to enhance the working conditions for subordinates thereby extracting optimum work out of them. There would be no point in extracting work from employees unless and until it is efficient to further the productivity, quality and quantity. Six Sigma provides tools that can be implemented to boost labour confidence and motivate them to better performance levels thus increasing not only their advancement but also elevates the company standards in the market.

Practical Aspects of Implementation

Managing finances is the basic aim of all non-manufacturing concerns. To maintain an organization's status is a difficult job and furthering its stand is a Herculean task. Without adequate finances the company cannot sustain itself and implementing Six Sigma would help in sorting out the accounting needs.

Six Sigma has chances of working wonders for the non-manufacturing sector if the managers and policy makers are more receptive towards changes and new conceptual ideas.

How to Overcome Six Sigma Controversies

"The more I learn about customer satisfaction, the less I know," the CEO of a FTSE 250 company recently lamented. By the time some companies get to understand their customers' needs fully, it will be too late. Management is often flooded with customer data detailing their satisfaction levels among other things; however, the data has been collected only as an exercise, not as a means to end customer dissatisfaction.

Can anyone Achieve Six Sigma?

There is no doubt that Six Sigma has enjoyed the seat of power like no other management tool has to date. The milestones crossed by the methodology are also non-controversial. Then where are there any problems and why is doubt being cast upon its ability to deliver?

Associate VP of a large software services company, a Champion and Master Black Belt himself, cites a major stumbling block for Six Sigma implementation, which is cultural change. A sudden change in the way people work and an altered reporting structure is what people find as obstructions to their routines. "Sometimes it takes ages to break this mindset", says another Six Sigma Black Belt who use to work with me.

Anyone that says they have successfully implemented Six Sigma means only that they have completed the implementation. It doesn't mean that they have actually achieved 3.4 defects per million. You will notice many things changing as you go about deploying Six Sigma. The market changes, you may see a change in technology or even an internal matter like organizational change can occur.

The Robust Mechanisms of Six Sigma

As with all other aspects of life, failures are always attributed to Six Sigma but not the successes. A successful Six Sigma implementation essentially requires a rock solid commitment from top management. Despite this, Six Sigma continues to question any authority, critically shaking most of the beliefs that the organization had about itself. As it goes deeper, it potentially shakes the foundations on which organizations exist.

The inordinate delay in data gathering is another obstacle to get Six Sigma out of the starting block. Sometimes the data is not divulged and other times it genuinely takes time to gather. Other priorities coupled with this pushes the implementation team to rush through the deployment.

Add to this the possibility of selecting the wrong project. If this happens, no matter how well you slog out later, the deployment will be a loser from the beginning. You will invariably fail to see a much different result from that of the original.

Indeed, it is the robust inbuilt mechanisms of Six Sigma that have worked for its success in almost all cases. One genuine concern about Six Sigma is about the cost of implementation, which very nearly challenges the ROI. As one CRM specialist put it, "where ROI has catapulted because of CRM, Six Sigma has been credited for it". This is the reason that Six Sigma is so widely accepted, despite the costs.

Chapter 7: Six Sigma and Business Continuity

So what is needed to use Six Sigma methodologies for improving business continuity? First, it's important to remember that Six Sigma is a customer-focused process improvement methodology. By contrast, the information technology (IT) environment tends to be service-oriented and an enabling function. This differentiates it from core processes, e.g., manufacturing, although IT is often a principal enabler of core processes.

Begin by recognising that:
1. Business continuity is a process.
2. It is customer-focused.
3. Its customers may need that process.

Break down business continuity into its component processes from start to finish. Depending on the level of detail, you may identify numerous sub-processes, such as "develop emergency team" or "conduct plan exercise". For these kinds of processes, ask your customers (of that particular process) what it is they want.

Next, have the project team measure the activity as a process performance. Let's look at a customer service centre as an example:

Customer requirements might be the following:
1. Availability (answer when called).
2. Response (do something when receiving a call).
3. Knowledgeable staff (address the situation during the call).

4. Safety (don't make the situation worse).
5. Follow-through (ensure satisfaction; collect payments).

The measurable performance criteria for this process might then be:
1. **Availability:** answer all calls between 0800 and 1800 within 30 seconds.
2. **Response:** log request and complete initial research for solution within one minute, take action within 10-30 minutes depending on the nature of the call.
3. **Knowledge of staff:** no returned calls needed, 98 percent of calls satisfied on first attempt.
4. **Follow-through:** all post-call activities completed within 5 minutes.

The principles of Six Sigma say that you should not have calls coming in to Customer Service. Instead, you should determine proactively why people are calling, and fix the root cause so they don't have to call in the first place!

What we all want, for example, is a computer that works all the time, is easy to use, does not fail, does what we expect, and when things go wrong, someone is there quickly to fix the problem. With some creative effort, it is possible to use the Six Sigma methodology with business continuity.

To overcome business continuity challenges, a business will be required to formulate emergency or disaster management plans, also referred to as business continuity. Further, businesses also need to ensure that the plans prove effective, for which they can use the highly effective concepts and methodologies of Six Sigma.

Six Sigma can certainly help in devising the most effective contingency plans because it follows a statistical approach for solving problems rather than using gut feelings that can prove to be wrong.

Employing DMAIC for Business Continuity

Most businesses nowadays are using the DMAIC (define, measure, analyze, improve, control) methodology for devising contingency plans for the future because the methodology is supposedly the best project management tool available. DMAIC was originally devised as a method for improving the efficiency of business processes, but now businesses are employing it for managing all types of projects, be it a quality improvement project or a business continuity project.

The DMAIC Process for Business Continuity

When DMAIC is being used for managing a business continuity project, the first step involves defining all the potential threats that can affect the company's productivity and profitability. Once the threats have been defined, the next step involves measuring the exact effects that each of these potential threats will have on the business. This is done with the help of advanced statistical tools and techniques or Six Sigma simulation software tools, all of which help in making the most accurate predictions.

After this, the project management team conducts a brainstorming session to analyze the threats in detail and to seek innovative and cost-effective solutions for dealing with such problems. To get better results, businesses need to ensure that suggestions and recommendations are solicited from experienced personnel working in different functional departments such as sales, purchase, warehousing, and others. This is necessary because the external threats not only have the potential to disrupt a company's production but can also have disastrous effects on the efficiency of other functional departments.

Based on the recommendations, improvements are then made wherever required across all functional departments. These improvement initiatives are aimed at either reducing or eliminating the potential damage that can occur in case the company were to face the threats for real. In the last phase of the DMAIC process, effective control systems are put in place so as to keep a regular check on the efficacy of improvements that were made earlier. Deploying control systems is necessary because disasters and contingencies can occur at any time and if the improvement measures are not up to mark, they will fail to provide the requisite level of security and protection.

Once all the requirements of DMAIC are met, a business needs to do nothing other than concentrate on its core processes, something that becomes a lot easier when both the external and internal threat perceptions have been eliminated with the help of business continuity plans.

Chapter 8: Six Sigma Makes Its Way to the Contact Centre

Contact Centres have benefited so much by implementing Six Sigma that now it is impossible for them to think that they can manage their operations without Six Sigma for a single day.

Why Six Sigma? Is Better Than Other Quality Initiatives?

Six Sigma may have been originally devised as a quality improvement tool for use in the manufacturing sector, but that has not stopped it from making its way to the services industry such as contact Centres. Six Sigma is different because it makes use of foolproof statistical tools and techniques that help in making the most accurate assessments, predictions and calculations, necessary for making effective and long-lasting quality improvements.

Six Sigma has stood the test of time when others have failed because it was quick to embrace emerging technologies, something that helped quite a bit in designing and developing newer and more effective quality improvement tools and techniques.

How is Six Sigma Helping Contact Centres?

Most contact Centres act as a vital link between a company and its customers. As such, it becomes quite important to provide high-quality services that will motivate customers to remain loyal to the company. By implementing Six Sigma,

Contact Centres have been able to achieve this objective quite easily, which in turn has proved beneficial for both the company and the customers.

Six Sigma has also helped to improve the efficiency of agents by reducing their workload and by providing improved work conditions to them.

How is Six Sigma Helping Contact Centres to Expand Their Operations?

Contact Centres that have implemented Six Sigma have saved millions of dollars over the years, which are now being used for expansion through the establishment of newer Contact Centres. Getting work for newly established Contact Centres is not a problem because every satisfied client automatically recommends the name of the contact Centre to other potential clients, bringing in more business for the Contact Centre.

Handling the increased workload is also not a problem because Six Sigma helps in streamlining operations so as to achieve optimum efficiency. Thus, we see that Six Sigma actually creates a highly profitable business cycle that can be used by any Contact Centre to expand its operations.

The Future of Six Sigma in Contact Centres

Six Sigma is probably the only quality improvement initiative that has survived the test of time. We can say with quite a lot of conviction that it will continue to be used by contact Centres as long as some other more effective quality improvement technique is not developed. The effectiveness of Six Sigma can be verified by the fact that companies that had implemented it ten to fifteen years back are still using it in spite of the huge changes in technology. After considering all these factors, it becomes much easier to predict the positive future of Six Sigma in Contact Centres.

Chapter 9: Six Sigma and Customer Relationship

Customer relationship management is one of the most important components of a successful business. Six Sigma provides business owners many valuable tools for measuring the relationship between customer and company in a way that allows changes to be made after the information that is collected is analyzed. In order to be successful, companies must establish a positive relationship with customers, one that will want to make them continue to purchase the products or services offered by the company.

Customer relationship management consists of several important factors. First, customer satisfaction must be established. In order for this to occur, there must be trust between customer and company. The customers must know the products or services they receive will be good quality and if there is a problem it will be taken care of professionally an in a timely manner. Six Sigma can be used to measure this, but it should be adhered to all the time in order to reach complete customer satisfaction.

Here the voice of the customer is used to designate the wants and needs customers experience. No matter what it is you are selling, you need to target your customers in a way that will make them keep coming back. By paying close attention to their wants and needs you can provide the products or services they have come to expect from your company.

There is much value built around customer satisfaction. The measurements that are used represent many different factors that are all components of customer satisfaction. If problems do occur, which they inevitably do at various points within the life of a company, the Six Sigma methods will help business owners figure out how to resolve them. This can also help company owners determine what problems might lie ahead so they can take care of them before they really present any risk.

Customer relationship management should be examined by teams that will perform various tests during the course of a particular Six Sigma project. The team members will use the information they are given to determine just what type of relationship customer and company have and how it can be improved over time. If there has been a certain amount of customer dissatisfaction, this will be evident in the data. This is what helps toward overall company improvement and keeps businesses running for many years

Six Sigma utilizes a customer centric approach for understanding the basic needs of the target audience. Understanding customer needs may seem to be an easy task, but in reality it is quite difficult because it calls for quantifying vague customer needs such as 'better quality', 'low price' and others into measurable terms. Six Sigma helps in proper assessment of customer needs because it is based on a data driven approach and makes use of statistical tools that give accurate results.

In the initial stages, a vast amount of data is collected based on the feedback provided by customers. For an existing product or service, the feedback may include improvement suggestions provided by customers - in the case of a new product launch, the feedback will include product features or preferences as suggested by the people belonging to the target audience.

The data is then categorized according to its relevance; for example, data related to the physical appearance of the product and data related to the features of the product are categorized under two different sections. Categorization is necessary as it helps to avoid confusion, which can occur any time due to the vast amounts of data that is being handled. After categorization, the data is analyzed with the help of statistical tools and the results or reports generated thereon are passed onto functional departments.

Satisfying Customer Needs

Once customer needs are quantified, the design team starts working on the product so as to make it more customer-friendly. In the case of an existing product, the design team suggests all the different alterations that can be made whereas in case of a new product, the design team creates the blueprint of different types of products having the same basic features. After this Six Sigma tools and techniques are used for selecting the best from amongst the available options based on their relevance to customer needs and the costs associated with the design and development of the product or service. The selected design or features are then put through further testing before making them available for actual production. With the help of Six Sigma testing tools, the design team can develop products that not only satisfy basic customer needs but also exceed their expectations.

Six Sigma goes a long way in determining the success of business organizations as it provides the necessary tools and techniques that help in increasing customer satisfaction. This in turn helps to develop customer loyalties, something that is vital for the long-term success of any business organization. Based on this, we can say with certainty that the scope of Six

Sigma is a lot more than just reducing defects or improving efficiencies.

Chapter 10: Transactional Six Sigma

Although Lean Six Sigma has its roots in traditional manufacturing, it also is helping to improve above-the-shop floor or so called back-office operations in those same organizations. Given its success in this transactional environment, the methodology is spilling over into services such as finance, public administration, transportation, education, customer service, insurance, and information technology.

Transactions are an integral part of business. Some transactions are simple, however most are complex and grow over time into unwieldy processes that are no longer competitive and drain resources. Insurance and banking transactions, for example, can take days or weeks to complete, resulting in customer dissatisfaction and extra costs.

In services, defects in transactional processes are difficult to identify and carry over into subsequent steps. In addition work-in-process (WIP) is concealed on computers and desks throughout the enterprise. Managers use Lean Six Sigma tools and its DMAIC roadmap to define, measure, analyze, improve, and control critical processes to deliver higher quality in less time.

There have been many debates and discussions among Six Sigma experts regarding the transactional costs and how Six Sigma strategies can be implemented to reduce the transactional losses.

There are 7 types of transactional costs.

1. **Search Costs:** Which tells a business how much searching for new suppliers and customers cost in time and money.

2. **Information Costs:** The costs that you have to incur for informing buyers about your product and quality and to know for yourself the potential customers and later customer details.

3. **Bargaining Costs:** The cost incurred for negotiating the terms of the sale. It depends a lot on the type of product or service that is being negotiated like for a multimedia CD the cost will be low but it will escalate when you are negotiating for a latest car model.

4. **Decision Costs:** There are considerable costs involved in the decision making process, such as the time and money spent to decide on buying a product.

5. **Policing Costs:** Again, there are substantial costs involved to ensure that the terms and conditions of sales and services are met.

6. **Enforcement Costs:** They are costs for resolving the unmet terms of sales and service as well.

7. **IT Costs:** The last cost that is not mentioned but should be invariably added in the list is the information technology cost. Information technology is something without which no company can carry out its day to day transactions of ordering, invoicing, purchasing, and payment processing. Therefore, the cost incurred on IT should also be taken into

consideration while making a list of transactional costs.

Different Products and Services but Same Transactions for All Business Organizations

Each business organization is unique in terms of the product or services that it offers but when it comes to internal operational and administrative transactions they are on same platform. All companies, whether they are categorized as manufacturing or service, have to take care of orders, issue invoices or bills, purchase supplies, write cheques, apply payments and handle all its financial transactions like any other business organization and even if the core of your business is a product or service, the key to making a profit lies in effective administration of transaction processing.

Speaking of financial transactions, your cash flow will also depend on following things:

1. **Accuracy:** In quantities, pricing, taxing etc and your cash flow will definitely suffer even if you made the perfect product but the customer demanded something else.

2. **Speed:** Speed matters when it comes to increasing the cash flow and it does not matter if you offer the best product of the world but if it takes unnecessarily long to get it ordered, delivered and installed, then customers won't wait for your product with bated breath. The transactions must be created and processed with quick precision and accuracy, along with having an extra team to fix an incorrect transaction on the spot if one arises.

3. **Cost:** Always keep an eye on the cost for creating and processing a transaction and the scrap and rework costs as well that occurs when an incorrect transaction is done.

Basic Tools of Six Sigma and Lean Six Sigma Used for Accelerating Cash Flow

1. **Tools of Six Sigma:** For finding and fixing errors on bills, orders etc make use of line, fishbone, and Pareto Six Sigma strategies. For monitoring the transactional error and cash flow, XmR chart can be used.

2. **Tools of Lean Six Sigma:** Lean Six Sigma will help you to find out and eliminate the delays in any transactional process that will additionally aggrandize your cash flow as well.

The conclusion that can be drawn from the above two points is that if you are only implementing Lean Six Sigma, then you will not be able to reduce defects in all processes. However, a combined effort can easily point out and rectify the errors in a transactional process.

Chapter 11: Using Six Sigma to Improve Office Processes

Using Six Sigma to improve office processes may be a relatively new phenomenon, but since the success rate of such quality improvement initiatives is high enough, it will not be wrong to proclaim that the future is certainly bright for such implementations.

Here, we look at how Six Sigma helping businesses to improve their office processes.

1. Defining Quality and Efficiency Standards

Six Sigma has made it a lot easier for business to define quality and efficiency standards as applicable to office processes, something that is a prerequisite for achieving the desired results. What Six Sigma does is that it converts vague quality and efficiency orders such as 'reduce errors', 'work fast' etc. into more definitive terms such as 'reduce errors by 15 percent in three months', 'process 20 files per hour' etc.

Now, all this new definitions may seem to be increasing the workload of employees, but that is certainly not true, because Six Sigma relies on time-tested tools and techniques that generate the most appropriate and realistic estimates of employee performance. In fact, employees stand to gain from such definitions because then they will know exactly what the company expects from them.

Additionally, since Six Sigma stresses replacing old inefficient systems with new newer, more efficient technologies, it is highly unlikely that the employees will have to do anything more than what they already might be doing. Businesses also stand to gain because then they can make accurate and timely predictions about human resource requirements.

This allows them to make the best possible use of existing resources, something that consequently results in huge cost savings.

2. Streamlining Existing Office Processes

Since office processes are quite different from manufacturing processes and since the human aspect needs to be given special consideration while initiating improvement measures in office processes, Six Sigma focuses on gathering input and feedback from employees before starting the tweaking process. Such input and feedback is gathered both at the time when the implementation team is in the process of selecting the right improvement methodology and when a methodology is finally short-listed for final implementation.

Getting such input and feedback is vital because it is the only way a business can possibly devise an improvement initiative that finds favour with the employees as well as gauge their initial reaction to a proposed improvement initiative. Since the success of such projects depends a lot on employee cooperation and support, it makes sense to take them into confidence right from the start. It is only then will the business be able to streamline its existing office processes without causing unnecessary employee disgruntlement or distrust, factors that are not conducive for the future growth prospects of any given business enterprise.

As we can see, Six Sigma does help a lot in improving the quality and efficiency of existing office processes, but what businesses should never forget is that employees are not machines that can be set to perform at specified levels of efficiency, all the time. As such, businesses need to adopt a more tolerant approach while using Six Sigma for improving their office processes.

Chapter 12: Measuring and Improving Service Processes with Six Sigma

They are a major part of the company's operating margins. The measurement, design and improvement of these processes are equally important parts of the Six Sigma initiative.

Defects and Metrics

The Six Sigma metrics used in the manufacturing industries are equally useful for the service sector. The metrics will change as per the service processes. The appropriate selection of the process, qualitative as well as quantitative, in the use of Six Sigma is necessary.

For example, while developing a website, certain factors like site design, colour schemes, user interaction and easy navigation need to be kept in mind. When Six Sigma concepts are applied to the site development process, all these variables will be examined for their effect on the customer and the ones that need improvement will be determined. It is a bit like carrying out a simple improvement in the manufacturing process.

Defects in the service sector can be defined as the problem in the process that leads to low customer satisfaction. Thee defects can be characterized as qualitative and quantitative. When a defect is measured quantitatively, it should also be converted into equivalent qualitative measures and vice versa.

For example, if the customer satisfaction for a service is being measured qualitatively, then it should also be converted to quantitative as 'satisfaction level' on a scale of 10. Below a certain level, the process needs improvement.

Another example is defining defects in quantitative measures, such as delivery services. For example, newspaper delivery has to happen before a certain time to be effective.

Measurements of Service Processes

1. **Level of measurement:** Using the appropriate level of measurement is very important for it to be useful and meaningful. For example, there may be 20 percent processes, which may be taking 80 percent of the total time of the project. When analyzing the qualitative measures, 20 percent of the customers may account for 80 percent of customer dissatisfaction (i.e. defects). The measurement of key areas, in contrast to detailed study, is necessary to get the larger picture of the process defects.

2. **Accounting for variations:** In service processes there are large numbers of variations that may arise, depending upon the complexity of the given task. The measurement of the typical task has to be done, as well as for special cases or situations that arise.

3. **Emphasize quantitative as well as qualitative measures:** A proper mix of the qualitative and the quantitative measures is very important to get useful results. A retailer's process, which has more personal customer contact, needs to measure the qualitative steps of the process. A company that provides

services where speed is relevant needs to concentrate more on the study of quantitative measures.

4. **Emphasize management communication and support:** In a service-based industry such as insurance, the claims process may have to be measured. There are different groups of people affected by the process who may resist any change. Management should communicate the relevance and effect of Six Sigma with the people involved to achieve the support for it.

As Six Sigma in service processes are linked to customer satisfaction ultimately leading to increase in sales, the need to measure and improve these processes is important.

Chapter 13: Improve Your Accounting Firm Processes

Poor processes directly affect client service and client satisfaction. You see it in delays in completing jobs, responding to client requests, or when a partner fails to communicate a piece of client-related information, causing an unnecessary mistake down the line. Inefficient processes can result in your firm's inability to bill for all the work in process, which decreases profitability. If your firm has experienced any of these problems, it is a sign of inefficient work processes that are keeping you from maximizing talents and resources. Lean Six Sigma, a method often used by manufacturers to improve internal processes, can improve your firm's business operations while driving short and long-term benefits to the bottom line.

In an accounting firm, Lean Six Sigma focuses on adding client value by eliminating non-value-added steps and inefficiencies in client service processes, resulting in more time to be proactive. It is a holistic, team-based approach that requires time and commitment to detect waste and inefficiency. Skilled facilitators (certified Black Belts who are trained experts in applying Lean Six Sigma concepts within an organization) lead teams through a thorough analysis of the "current state" of the firm's processes. Waste and inefficiencies are identified, and lean techniques (tools that are focused on process effectiveness and understanding client value) are applied to eliminate waste and improve processes.

Lean Six Sigma in Action: Tax Practice Example

The accounting firm I work with in 2011; a USA based CPA firm embraced this approach in its quest to better serve clients and to become an improved trusted adviser firm. I led the firm through a Lean Six Sigma tax program beginning in the fall of 2011. Initially, we had about a year of startup costs, including tuition for the Black Belt and Master Black Belt program, initial test project and modifying of the improvement model specific to a CPA firm. Starting with a handful of their offices in the fall of 2011, we slowly rolled out a Lean Six Sigma tax program. We saw enough gains and benefits to warrant a firm-wide rollout beginning in the fall of 2012.

Much of the waste in tax processes is viewed as small in nature and therefore overlooked. Nearly every step of a process has some form of waste; it is important to identify this (however small) and be able to quantify it to show the entire impact to the process. Before you know it, "minor" wastes can add up to 20% or 30% inefficiency. Lean Six Sigma seeks to identify and quantify globally these wastes and implement simple solutions to drastically improve the effectiveness of the overall process.

Type of Waste

To make lasting improvements, everyone at the firm had to thoroughly understand the impact of poor processes on the firm and clients. When looking at their business tax process, for example, several areas of inefficiency were identified. They fell into the categories of waste that are standard in Lean Six Sigma.

1. **Defects:** Following the 80-20 principle, by identifying and focusing on the 20% of mistakes that generated the most delays, 80% of the time the reviewer and tax preparer needed to make corrections before completing the return was reduced.

2. **Overproduction:** Jobs were ineffectively prioritized. Excessive time and resources were used during the heart of busy season to work on clients that file extensions every year. Instead of focusing on what needed to be done at that moment to effectively take care of the client from an extension and estimated payment standpoint more work was being done on the return. Meanwhile, other clients waited.

3. **Waiting:** Wait times, a symptom of bottlenecks, were found at several steps, including first review. A "learning curve" was identified; the longer something stayed in the review queue, the more time the preparer needed to become reacquainted with the client and the thought process that took place during the previous touch.

    Not utilizing people's talents. Partners did too many administrative activities, did too much project management and spent too much time in the minutiae. They were not staying at a high level and focusing on ways to better serve clients. Younger team members were not being developed, stretched and trusted.

4. **Transporting:** Too many paper folders were being transferred throughout offices, resulting in time

delays. Individuals weren't optimally located to work with their primary teams.

5. **Inventory:** Excess work in process occurred. This led to a lot of started and partially completed work, but fewer finished products getting out the door to clients. Bottlenecks and delays in client service were also created.

6. **Motion:** Hard copies and electronic copies of documents were not being filed properly. This led to "Easter egg hunts" in which time was wasted searching for certain pieces of information or communication.

7. **Excess processing:** Time was spent outside the scope of the engagement on things such as cleaning up bookkeeping and fixing mistakes. People didn't realize the scope of an engagement and performed more work than the client engaged the firm to do and was willing to pay for. Put simply, the firm wasn't matching client expectations of the scope of the engagement.

8. **Attitude:** If each office developed its own process, consistency would not be viewed as important. By unveiling a consistent, firm-wide process, everyone understood the benefits of Lean Six Sigma, such as improving profitability and work/life balance. Attitudes changed and individual employees adopted a one-process mindset regardless of location.

To improve the results, we must first define some new metrics:

1. **Voice of the client:** The lean concept of efficiency and client value is based on understanding what the client desires. The client is both internal (the next person in your firm to touch the service after you) and external (the person who receives the final product). You must ensure that your firm's processes can meet their demands.

2. **Value-added and non-value-added steps:** Look at value through the eyes of your internal and external clients. Non-value-added steps do not contribute to the satisfaction, needs or qualities desired by the client. An analysis of value-added vs. non-value-added time in processes is a must.

3. **Lead time:** This is the entire time from when the clients' work comes in the door until the work is complete. Your firm can gain efficiency by reducing the lead time (which differs from cycle time below).

4. **Cycle time:** Cycle time is the time a project is actually in process. Cycle time starts when the client's work is picked up and ends when the final product is delivered. Don't confuse this with lead time. Lead time includes the time before cycle time; when the project was dropped off. If you don't have all the info you need from the client upfront, this will add to both the lead time and cycle time.

5. **Review notes:** The level and number of review notes can also help measure efficiency. This data typically exists in the mind of a partner and isn't tracked. It is a valuable way to improve your processes and gauge your improvements.

6. **Chargeable hours:** One final measure of process efficiency is reducing your chargeable hours; taking less time to do more work. Historically, chargeable hours have been an inefficient metric for CPA firms to use when gauging effectiveness because it promotes the wrong behaviour. If you ask for chargeable hours, you will get chargeable hours; but those hours may not be efficient or productive. The mantra in your firm should be to reduce your chargeable hours and become more effective unless you are growing your client base at a rate of 20% or more, for example, which would of course mean that you would not be reducing chargeable hours.

7. **Traditional metrics:** Besides chargeable hours, other traditional metrics can still be used to judge the success of a Lean Six Sigma project. The CPA tax division experienced the following results during the 2013 tax season; realization (amount billed/WIP) increase of 6% year over year, chargeable hours decrease of 7.5% and a 2% increase in revenue all amid the worst recession in 25 years.

Lessons Learned

Throughout the lean process, the firm learned many things that may apply to all CPA firms:

Technology doesn't always help efficiency. Throwing technology at a process isn't the complete answer. Software best practices tend to be one-size-fits-all and, if they have not been optimally integrated to your global process, you won't see much of an increase in efficiency, despite the salesperson's best pitch. The Firm struggled internally with software rollouts in the past because processes were not aligned with the new software, resulting in loss of effectiveness and efficiency. The process is the backbone of a firm, while technology is a tool to help the process. You have to understand how the software fits into an optimal overall process not how the process can fit into the technology. Many firms go awry by allowing software to drive their processes, rather than aligning it with existing needs, resulting in an enhanced process.

Throwing manpower at a non-bottleneck step doesn't help. Hiring additional resources to prepare tax returns increased the volume of returns at the review stage. Since the number of reviewers didn't change, only a finite number of tax returns could be reviewed each day. Therefore, the bottleneck increased at the review stage. Resource redeployment was key to improving this inefficiency. Firms are wasting money adding resources in non-bottleneck steps and not fixing the process.

Failure to engage the work force. For effective, efficient processes to be developed, you need input from the front lines. Using a top-down approach, like a small management team dictating procedures, will not generate the buy-in you need.

Getting Started with Lean and Six Sigma

To get started we used the following tools. These can be big contributors to success before delving into the changes that impact actual work product.

1. **Identify internal customers:** Identify the needs of your internal customers and make sure your processes

support them. You can't have 100% external client satisfaction if you don't focus on having 100% internal customer satisfaction.

2. **Increase work flow:** A value stream map (similar to a workflow chart with various types of process shapes connected by arrows) can help identify value-added vs. non-value-added steps. The map can also provide those involved with a common language or reference point when working through improvement ideas. Your process will flow better after identifying and eliminating non-value-added steps, bottlenecks and the potential for errors.

3. **Assign a champion:** By picking a person in each office, work team or group to participate in ongoing workflow analysis, you can level the workload and respond to client needs in a timely and effective way. Champions also encourage continual improvement of your processes.

4. **Improvement through DMAIC Model (a Six Sigma concept). Define, measure, analyze, improve and control the process:** By using a cross-functional team, you can promote continual improvement. Start by Defining your project. Determine who is on the team and their roles, list objectives, and define the scope of the project. Next, Measure how the work currently flows through the process. This helps to identify the preliminary sources of waste. Then, analyze the current state. Put the steps under the microscope and zoom in on your wastes and inefficiencies. Only after thorough analysis can you work to improve the process. Implement

simple, targeted solutions to eliminate waste and improve effectiveness. Keep in mind your top priority to better serve client needs. Lastly, Control the process by documenting the procedures, providing training and getting everyone on board with the new way of working.

Final Result

Lean Six Sigma can be an effective tool for improving the efficiency of your firm's processes. Viewed holistically, this approach can help your firm objectively review and improve the processes your team performs every day.

With the appropriate time and commitment from all levels of your firm, your firm can enjoy the benefits distinguishing itself from the competition by providing better value to its employees and clients. If you do what you have always done, you will get the same results. Make a change. Get results.

Chapter 14: Six Sigma in Healthcare

Six Sigma methodologies aim at improving overall quality by eliminating defects and achieving near perfection by restricting the number of possible defects to less than 3.4 defects per million. In the services sector, Six Sigma concepts are used mainly for eliminating transactional errors.

Today, the concepts and methodologies of Six Sigma are increasingly being used in the healthcare industry for improving the quality of services rendered, increasing efficiency, and eliminating human errors that can often prove fatal. However, the use of Six Sigma in the healthcare industry is a relatively new phenomenon as compared to other service industries that have undergone some type of data-supported, systematic, quality-improvement process. With medical and technological advancements, the demand and expectations for improved medical care are continuously increasing. However, due to lack of effective management systems, inefficiency is increasing, which often leads to congested emergency rooms, customer complaints, and lost revenues.

Benefits

Six Sigma concepts and methods enable a healthcare organization to offer improved healthcare services to patients by streamlining business processes. In the healthcare industry, the quality of services rendered depends a lot on human skills, which is often very difficult to measure and control. Six Sigma is effective as it is based on a comprehensive approach that focuses on improving both human as well as transactional aspects of a process. Although implementing Six

Sigma concepts in the healthcare industry is a challenging task, it does help in getting quick results.

In the healthcare industry, the factors that determine the quality and efficiency are usually the flow of information and interaction between people. Six Sigma helps in streamlining the flow of information and achieving strategic business results by initiating cultural shifts all throughout the organization. Six Sigma focuses on improving processes rather than just concentrating on the task, which helps in increasing the scope of improvements. It provides the necessary tools and methodologies that help in analyzing and transforming human performance, necessary for achieving significant long-term improvements.

Process

Six Sigma helps in defining a vision for the future, identifying specific goals, and establishing quantitative measures for turning that vision into reality. It helps in formulating goal plans and setting timelines for moving from current performance levels to Six Sigma performance levels. The plans are defined only after documenting their effects on the organization's work processes' that may include flow of information, surgical site procedures, handling patients, and others.

The basic requirements for successfully implementing Six Sigma programs are usually long-term vision, commitment, leadership, management, and training. It is important to provide the requisite training to doctors, nurses, and the administrative staff for making them aware about the various concepts and methodologies. The training may initially appear to be expensive, but is often worth the cost when one considers the benefits such as improved quality of services and increased efficiency. It is necessary for employees working in a healthcare organization to develop an understanding about the various Six Sigma concepts. This will help them in integrating new techniques into the Six Sigma processes for improving quality and effectiveness.

Six Sigma Project Reduces Analytical Errors in an Automated Lab

As part of the laboratory's ongoing performance-improvement process, changed results had been measured for years. Although the average percentage of changed results was consistently below 1% in the three main areas of the laboratory - hematology, coagulation, and chemistry; the administration had noted that eight analytical process failures had occurred in the first half of 2003, resulting in the correction of reported values that affected multiple patients at one time.

The problem was sporadic; there was no clear solution; and correcting the issue would help achieve the core lab's goal of improving patient care, increasing customer satisfaction, and boosting staff moral. The core lab's administration believed that reducing the number of failed analytical processes was a worthy goal for a Six Sigma project. A multidisciplinary team of technical management, information systems staff, and physicians assembled to tackle the problem using the Six Sigma using define, measure, analyze, improve, and control (DMAIC) approach.

Six Sigma methodology

Six Sigma, a focused, high-impact process, uses proven quality principles and techniques to reduce process variance, and seeks to confine errors to 3.4 defects per million opportunities (DPMO). Six Sigma relies on rigorous statistical methods and implements control mechanisms in order to tie together quality, cost, process, people, and accountability, and begins with an understanding of customer requirements and values (referred to as voice of the customer). Once these are defined, Six Sigma's process enables the identification of factors critical to customer satisfaction. The processes involved in these critical factors are then analyzed and measured. Improvement strategies are focused on the vital "X." The Six Sigma goal is to reduce both variance and control processes in order to assure compliance with the critical specifications.

Defining and measuring the process

During the define phase, the Six Sigma team developed a high-level process map with the initial step being preparation of the analyzers for use and the final step being release of the result. The project's scope covered the process from sample placement on the analyzer to the point at which the result was released in the LIS. A defect was defined as the need to change a result for any reason after verification.

Also during the define phase, the Six Sigma team needed to convince lab employees that further reduction of changed results was necessary, even though the average changed-result rate was already less than 1%. To accomplish this, the team used change acceleration process tools, such as the threat/opportunity matrix, to demonstrate the benefits of reducing changed results and the disadvantages of maintaining the current changed-result rate. For instance, reducing changed results would increase lab efficiency, improve staff performance and moral and boost market share. Maintaining the current rate of changed results would ultimately diminish the core lab's reputation, leading to a loss of revenue and decreased staff moral.

In the measure phase, the Six Sigma team used operational definitions and the lab supervisory staff to perform measurement-system analysis. Because the lab already operated at a high sigma level, the measurement system had to be 100% accurate for reproducibility and repeatability. The team had to ensure that any variations were due to the process, not the measurement system. In order to obtain this type of accuracy, the team developed operational definitions to classify errors: procedural, auto-verification, sample, clerical, mechanical, and unknown. With the aid of logic trees, the team refined these definitions five times to ensure all errors were classified consistently so that repeatability and reproducibility were 100%. Statistical analysis using the Six Sigma methodology revealed that the lab operated at a 4.8 sigma level.

For the period of May 2003 through July 2003, the laboratory corrected 585 test results out of 1,645,975 results reported. The DPMO was 355. One of the Six Sigma tools; the stakeholder analysis aided in developing a strategy to gain support for the project from moderately opposed individuals and helped identify those individuals likely to be involved in the process who could serve as resources for the team.

Analyzing and improving procedures

In the analyze phase, the Six Sigma team developed its aggressive goal of reducing analytical errors by 35% to a DPMO of 230 and a sigma score of 5.0. As the process moves toward a sigma level between 5 and 6, eliminating defects without eliminating the human factor becomes increasingly difficult.

Graphical analysis using Pareto charts indicated 86% of the defects could be attributed to two types of errors: Whereas 52% of the defects were procedural errors committed by employees while reviewing results, 34% of the defects were the result of auto-verification errors by the LIS. This discovery was enlightening; SOPs (standard operating procedures) were not accomplishing their intended goals.

Six Sigma focuses on process, not people. Before the analysis, the team members had been convinced the culprit was something beyond the core lab's control, such as unacceptable specimens received from the rapid response labs or from the outreach physician's office. The lab had established SOPs for all operations, yet the staff was having difficulty making key decisions when it came to releasing analytical results. The analysis of variance (ANOVA) proved this vital "X" to be statistically significant. The null hypothesis that all types of analytical errors are the same was rejected because the p-value 0.001 was less than 0.05; thus, the team could conclude that a statistical difference in the number of defects existed among the different error categories.

The team utilized tools like failure mode and effect analysis (FMEA) to break down the very complicated process into individual steps; potential failure modes, effects, severity, cause, occurrence, control, and detection, so its members could look at key drivers, or "Xs," in the process. Data for each step was analyzed graphically and tested mathematically for statistical significance.

One vital "X" was that the majority of errors occurred on two analyzers; general chemistry and hematology. The team drilled down, utilizing the five why's tool and the voice of the customer from the technical staff. By developing an assessment tool, the team identified deficiencies in the staff training program. Staff trained by the vendor or lab supervisors scored 40 points higher on competency tests than peer-trained staff. The result was obvious. Ongoing basic training needed to be performed to stress analyzer maintenance, troubleshooting, and recognition of analyzer "flags."

To reduce the number of procedural errors in the improve phase, a simplified result-review guideline tool was provided to technologists as an aid in the critical decision-making process used to validate test results. The auto-verification process was modified to capture real-time suspect flags for CBC orders; results that required review were held by the LIS. The LIS team designed software that enabled real-time analyzer-result monitoring for chemistry analyzers, complete with an audio alert for notification of potential problems.

Controlling results

In the control phase, the Six Sigma team implemented a plan that incorporated individual and moving range charts for monitoring corrected results. The control plan enabled the team to determine the method for monitoring frequency, alert flag, action, and specific accountability for each of the key variables in the process. The DPMO for corrected results is now monitored on a monthly basis. The Six Sigma metric has become part of the lab's quality-management program. Real-life examples of analyzer printouts and flag results are used to assess staff competency on an ongoing basis.

At the end of the control phase, the process went from a 4.8 sigma level to a 5.0 sigma level. Using the chi-square test, the team was able to demonstrate a statistically significant decrease in the number of corrected results. The technical area of the core lab has experienced a 20% growth in volume from the completion of the project in December 2003 to present. The Six Sigma team turned the project over to its process owner in January 2004. Since that point, the department has operated at a sigma level of 5.0 or higher and was at a 5.2 sigma level as of October 2004. This project produced no direct financial impact. The error-reduction project was undertaken because it was the right thing to do.

The Six Sigma DMAIC methodology has many advantages. It is a rigorous process that engages front-line employees in process redesign. It utilizes data and the voice of the customer to determine the factors that are most critical to quality. Controls and accountability are put in place to ensure the process remains efficient. Finally, this approach provides lab personnel with the tools to take a good process and make it even better.

Chapter 15: Improve Your Bottom Line

Very easily, Six Sigma is your best bet for maximizing return on investment, more so in troubled economic times. However, the success of implementation depends much on its achieved degree of alignment with the problems. Ifs and buts notwithstanding, there are stories to support both sides of the issue. First let's consider the negative side of the story.

Why do we Hear Failures to Achieve Projected ROIs (Return On Investment) on Six Sigma Investments?

We hear failure stories not just because they are reported but because they occur. Now, why do they occur so much as to be heard in the open? The first reason any practitioner can give is the lack of support from the top management. Considering long implementation periods, commitment levels sometimes wither away and consequently the effects percolate down the line of the organization and project implementation turns into a ritual exercise. The claims of $1 million per Black Belt in ROI can appear more and more unrealistic. It is not enough to blame top management alone. Champions and Master Black Belts on their parts could scale down the projects that result in slashed expenses. High returns can be realized in this scenario by driving projects initially through the internal market to gain much-needed support. Things are subjective to multiple aspects but a complete turnaround is not impossible.

What Critical Factors Help Bring About Satisfactory ROI?

There are three more critical factors barring project selection that play a role in ROI. Obviously, these are:
1. Lowering the investment.
2. Maximizing the returns.
3. Reducing the time to return.

But things are more complex than meets the eye! Interrelated variables such as quality of personnel and Six Sigma training, support of management and magnitude of the opportunity, function in unison. Apart from these, aligning the management (and stakeholders') initiatives to the Six Sigma initiatives must be given due importance. All good programs will launch from a project on revenue maximization that potentially becomes an instant hit.

How to Measure ROI in a Six Sigma Initiative?

Return on investment simplistically means the cost of implementation over time compared to return for the corresponding period after discounting inflation and risk adjusted rates. For reasons of practicality, return on investment is measured in terms of hard and soft returns. Hard returns are those which are tangible and can be measured; for example, the savings achieved on reduced personnel and wastage. Whereas soft returns are mostly intangible like the advantage derived from the reduced cycle time.

Soft returns vary hugely from company to company and from project to project, unlike hard returns, which are measured almost by the same yardstick universally. So clearly, the soft returns are relative in nature, depending on accepted interpretations at that time, thus making quantification a difficult exercise. Errors in calculation of reduced capital employed or cost of financing leaves tremendous room for debate.

As a rule, most successful companies don't differentiate between hard and soft returns. What is more interesting is the recurring returns in terms of all around savings. Add to it the value creation by increases in the growth rates and defeating competition, which all result in higher shareholder value.

More sophisticated tools such as Economic Value Analysis may help quantify intangible value created.

Chapter 16: Six Sigma Assessment

Assessing Six Sigma is not end of the process post implementation, although an analysis of a failed Six Sigma project points out the lack of commitment by upper management and lack of attention to the cultural and business investment required for accomplishing and sustaining new tiers of performance. It is in this context that assessment of Six Sigma becomes necessary, especially when new attempts by companies on improvement projects, reveal that the journey will be long and hard.

Assessing the Different Implementation Stages of Six Sigma

The key to the success of Six Sigma implementation lies in assessing the status quo at various stages. Assessments reveal the deviations the implementation efforts have taken from the intended line of progress. As the deployment of Six Sigma is signified by emphasis on accomplishing benchmarks in process optimization and control to render progressively higher degrees of quality, performance efficiency and timeliness, a system of assessment needs to be inbuilt which puts in place an appropriate set of checks and balances.

Six Sigma Assessment Procedures

There has not been a single assessment procedure either devised or used by any one company which applies to all processes and industries. Companies successful at their Six Sigma implementation have developed and adopted their own assessment procedures. Some of them have used their own internal audit teams with their own criteria to assess the progress of Six Sigma implementation. Many Six Sigma companies have actually gone ahead with evolving a custom developed audit system based on ISO 9000.

The Assessment Categories in Six Sigma

The fundamental premise of assessment in Six Sigma is identifying and reading the gaps between 'as is' and 'should be' conditions of the process stages. The 'should be' list of conditions is what is established at the beginning of the deployment described in great length for each category. The categories for assessment are listed below:
1. Leadership
2. Communication and Implementation in Everyday Activities
3. Project Effectiveness and Efficiency
4. Organizational Transformation
5. Customer Impact

The requirements of these top level categories are the customized topics needed for achieving overall objectives. The method of assessment contains written tests and interviews starting with top level managers down to line employees, in addition to meetings and seminars.

The overall results are shown as applicable to the core business process. The results of leadership assessments that show possible areas for improvements are essentially helpful in chalking out a course correction plan. The results also show weaknesses that are to be assessed as the first step toward fine tuning the exercise for needed changes.

The need for assessment may be fulfilled whenever it is warranted. In the normal course, where the results take 4-6 months to show, the assessment can be scheduled as an annual exercise. Experience from successful implementation of Six Sigma has shown that major roadblocks in changing an organizational mind set lies in sustaining the gains made.

Chapter 17: How to Measure Innovation in Your Business

Traditionally, these elements have consisted of counting defects, measuring costs, and tracking cycle times. Today, as we understand businesses processes better, it has become a bit more involved but no less achievable.

With improvement strategies such as Six Sigma a set of techniques that focuses on the process of improvement within a business there are ample measures available to recognize if your business is achieving its potential, or if it is lacking on one or many levels.

There are primarily five areas of measure for innovation, which include:
1. **Performance:** Our company's ability to provide a total solution in relation to its requirements and its competition.
2. **Quality:** The number of defects and the number and rate of delay.
3. **Timing:** Its speed to the market, including its schedule for internal development (also known as cycle time) and its external market timing.
4. **Finances:** Revenue expectations, costs, margins.
5. **Development costs:** For specific projects.

Additionally, there are a number of sub-categories for measuring innovation within your business. These include:
1. Turnover of personnel.
2. Percentage of product and/or service tests passed.

3. Percentage of reuse (the number of tested items that were borrowed).
4. Number of specification or requirement changes needed.
5. Percentage of new parts (the number of items that are untested).
6. Percentage of unique parts (potential areas for difficulty in integration).
7. Percentage of new vendors.
8. Percentage of staffed to plan (including times of over-staffing and under-staffing).
9. Percentage of designated time lost to undesignated projects.

As you can see, there is quite a bit to consider when you wish to measure the innovation of your business. This often explains the inclination for businesspeople to put off such measurements. However, by doing so, you are only holding back from the ideas, changes, and potential that you could be offered from the result of these measurements. The best time for you to measure the innovation of your business is today.

Chapter 18: Synchronize Six Sigma into Your Business

What leadership must keep in mind when deciding on Six Sigma is its ability to solve the most difficult problems. However, commoditization and variability in deployment have been the stumbling blocks for success. "Dumbing Down" of the methodology and displacing it as a tool of decision making which is aided by the critical thinking process and losing customer focus will only contribute to the acceleration of its demise. If things are not put into proper perspective, the metrics for its goal measurement, which is maximization of bottom line or savings, loses focus.

Phases in Synchronizing Six Sigma

Six Sigma can be synchronized with business processes in three phases. The phases can be modified based on the suitability.

1. **Initialization Phase:** The various steps can be summarized as follows:
   a. Identifying and apportioning of enterprise level savings goal with SBUs.
   b. Identifying Champions and aligning compensations to attainment of goals.
   c. Establishment and streamlining of the steering committee and reporting channels.
   d. Writing down and aligning the deployment plan with a highlighted financial savings plan.
   e. Communicating and preparing the workforce to deployment.

2. **Execution Phase:** This is the crucial phase in the implementation. The project progress decides the direction in which it is moving:
   a. All key data are communicated, through a designated database, to upper management for continuous review.
   b. Champions engage X-belts to gauge progress to ensure mentoring.
   c. Regular monitoring and reviews at business meetings.
   d. Delays are discussed and dealt with according to necessities. They are terminated, postponed or extended with additional resources as may become necessary.
   e. Steering committees at SBU and corporate levels assess progress towards stated goals and day to day benefits and prioritize new projects for assignment to the Belts.
   f. Project teams are individually acknowledged for their accomplishments and rewarded.
   g. X-belts prepare document of implementation as knowledge notes for records and future references.
   h. Champions report to accountable executives in the management

3. **Assessment Phase:** Assessment is done at least once a year to assess the progress and quantify the figures.
   a. Promotes greater and earlier alignment by accelerating result generation and sustainability.
   b. Emphasis is placed on real versus theoretical or anecdotal data.
   c. Focus will be placed on capturing benefits, enhancing the belts' performance and certification, deployment planning, and overall performance.

d. SBUs are informed of results relative to the organization.

e. Steering committees revisit the deployment plan with a view to revise as may be necessary.

f. Training for Belts or refresher workshops, and reorientation for Master Black Belts and Champions who undergo certification program are scheduled.

g. Rescheduling, if necessary, of early sustainability by "training the trainer".

Like implementation, synchronization is a continuous process as seen above until self-sustainability and goals are achieved. Benefits can be realized with perseverance by all those involved throughout its implementation.

Chapter 19: Voice of the Customer

Six Sigma places highest priority on customer data input which provides the much-needed insight into what the customers need and what he or she is thinking about the products already on the market as a measure of performance. The design team needs to understand the requirements of the customer and predict whether the proposed (or the existing) design meets customer expectations.

How is Customer Satisfaction Ensured?

All business activities are customer centric. Even the best product may not sell if it possesses useless value for the customers. A point in the case is the satellite phone Irridium that Motorola developed some time ago. Although it was the first and the best in its class, it failed in the market because the customer did not find any value in that particular product.

1. Customer's Experience of Defects and Costs

Customers have a different perspective about quality and cost. The variation in satisfaction levels across different market segments and regions needs to be analyzed as a first step towards reaching goals. In Six Sigma, customer input, however scattered it may be, when analyzed can be categorized making way for an in-depth understanding of company goals.

2. Product Relevance

The relevance of any product to the customer stems from its utility, cost and quality. A robust design is not just strong but simple, flexible and idiot-proof. It consistently produces a high level of performance despite huge variations in manufacturing and customer needs. Anything not adding value will not get customer attention.

3. Adjusting Process Capability to Customer Requirements

The need for adjusting the process capability is basically considered in DMAIC (a Six Sigma methodology for existing products), without putting significant burden on the cost. This begins with estimation of financial impact, feasibility studies of the technicalities involved and market uptake. The outcome of these studies will guide any process adjustments.

4. Controlling Process Variations

The uncertainties of processing are the variation that needs to be tackled as a critical step in achieving the 3.4 defect threshold. Uncertainties arise mainly due to a huge number of key elements in a process, outdated process steps and lack of control. Variability surrounding a product or process can be rooted out at the design and analytical stages.

5. Removing Roadblocks

The roadblocks for Six Sigma Implementation can sometimes be within the organization, such as trans-jurisdictional roadblocks which sometimes threaten the effective implementation of Six Sigma. The Black Belts need Champions' intervention in removing these roadblocks.

6. Hitting the Finish line

Taking Six Sigma to its logical conclusion is no small matter, even for cash rich corporations. The millions of dollars that it takes for Six Sigma implementation and the long cycle for the results to show can unsettle even the strongest organizations. Finishing the task, despite allotment of huge funds, accessibility to knowledge base, depends primarily on the commitment level of senior leadership and a dedication to customer satisfaction.

Chapter 20: Benefits of Six Sigma Certification

Will it Really Benefit Your Organization?

The success of Six Sigma Certification and implementation depends on many factors. It requires nothing less than a relentless effort and dedication to see that it succeeds. Although specific procedures may be in place, an equal responsibility lies on upper management to dedicate 100% of their time and resources to this mammoth task. The top and bottom ends of your business, and all those in between, need to come together with single minded contributions to make Six Sigma certification and implementation successful.

You need to realize that, before the real implementation begins with Six Sigma methodology, the groundwork needs to be laid. Depending on the size and culture of your business, your team needs to have a brainstorming session, with key focus on potential benefits and consequences of having your employees attain Six Sigma certification. As the employer, you need to sponsor your employees in their Six Sigma training efforts. The decision to go for Six Sigma certification is nothing less than a dollars and cents decision.

Benefits to Your Business

Six Sigma certification benefits are both tangible and intangible. Intangible benefits can be in the form of customer loyalty that will follow the life of your business. Below we examine some of the benefits of Six Sigma certification.

1. Increase in Your Bottom Line

Six Sigma certification results in improved processes, better utilization of resources like finances, time and materials and reduction in the cost of production. On the customer side, there is higher satisfaction with products/services. This improves your bottom line substantially.

2. Increases Shareholder Value

Fundamentally, this results from increased revenues, but in addition to this, there is increased customer loyalty and confidence that raises the stock values as well as the value to shareholders (to whom you are responsible).

3. Total Customer Satisfaction

Customers get more than what they asked for on the product/service side, at a lower price or higher value.

4. Decreased Employee Attrition

Six Sigma training boosts employee moral due to a reduced workload. Six Sigma certified employees realize the positive returns of quality work, which keeps them motivated. This reduces employee turnover and burnout.

5. Six Sigma Certification Creates a Win-Win Situation for the Supply Chain

In converting supplier-customer relationships to long-term partnerships, both parties win. Six Sigma training and certification accelerates this process with its focus on quality, prices come down and both the product quality and life cycle time improve.

Chapter 21: Conclusion

Managing a business in any industry is especially difficult to keep up with on various levels. People usually find that they are unable to balance their obligation to a productive and proficient operating model while still ensuring they have access to as much growth and profitability as possible. Anyone considering a Lean Six Sigma effort should know the basics of successfully implementing these management principles as part of making sure their efforts are well coordinated.

Lean Six Sigma management practices are designed to help businesses implement the most productive and failure proof operations possible throughout their organization. Companies are often interested in this particular model when attempting to ensure their efficiency levels and overall cost control needs are as carefully managed as possible at all times. Businesses considering the implementation of this model are quite specific in their efforts.

Any company that is considering lean concepts is faced with a wealth of opportunities for success. Many leaders are uncertain of where to even initiate their first steps while being assured their needs are fully met. Concentrating on numerous factors is actually quite helpful in making sure the program is as well managed as possible.

Leaders should initially be certain they fully comprehend all the principles and guidelines that are associated with this management practice through proper training for both themselves and their employees. The various guidelines and principles that govern this process are based on the need to be assured that all phases of implementation are accurate and appropriate for their organization. Specific training courses and certifications are readily available for leaders to participate in that are actively considering this particular option.

Another source of consideration in this effort is concentrating on the use of specifically trained consultants. Hiring a consultant is often a beneficial idea when implementing any kind of quality control program as they are typically versed in highly specialized forms of operations that are helpful to companies. Many professionals only charge a fee for their services if they are effective in providing guidance to their clients.

Companies should also make sure their employees are fully trained on all principles that are being discussed and considered. People often discover that employees are typically uncertain of what should be focused on throughout their daily routines when attempting to assist in implementing a lean strategy. Proper training and clear delegation of responsibilities helps ensure that everyone is on board with what is required of them.

Leaders are also required to be certain their employees have the appropriate tools to perform their jobs. Successfully keeping up with daily operations is reliant on the need to ensure that workers are fully prepared to do their jobs in an efficient capacity. Any new tools required for productive operations should be readily focused on as needed.

Implementing Lean Six Sigma management principles requires consistent hard work. The factors that are often focused on by businesses include making sure that metrics are weighed against actual performance. Accurately and consistently keeping track of the operations avoids lacklustre results that are often distracting from overall output.

Keep Improving!!!

www.ingramcontent.com/pod-product-compliance
Lightning Source LLC
Chambersburg PA
CBHW051723170526

45167CB00002B/779